Praise for Fr

Stories collide, contrast, and gro
elegant new collection. Voices a
their right to exist in an overload
images that whipped by in fast succession as if blown by a wind of
crackling static." Yet, meaning is also found in this mélange of thoughts
and stories we call life. "Lead me into a new day   into that particular
specificity of light," the poet demands. We can all support one another that
way if we follow Ilechko's inspired instructions.

> Anatoly Molotkov, Co-Editor at the Inflectionist Review,
> and the author of several books

"I have nothing new to tell you   nothing that is previously unheard"
writes Paul Ilechko, in his wonderfully inventive book "Fragmentation and
Volta." And while that may be true (though debatable), Ilechko journeys
through fractals of imagining, with a riveting push for revelation. I could
say much about the craft in this book. How Ilechko uses caesura as fine-
tuned as Merwin did, or how he's accomplished poetry as Impressionism.
But that would be a grave disservice. These pages make me feel alive,
celebrated in my flawed humanity. They harness ghosts, confession,
homage, "the stank of smoke and memories," a stubborn hope.

> Luke Johnson, 2024 California Book Award Finalist
> and author of *Quiver* (Texas Review Press, 2023) and
> *Distributary* (Texas Review Press, 2025)

This book wonderfully weaves memory, metaphor, and rich imagery into
moments that act like a field guide to the unconscious. The poet explores
loss and regret with language that's tactile and a touch that's universal.
Here you'll also find jagged lives and landscapes, particularly in the prose
"Fragments" sections of the book. These poems understand the balance in
how "the failure / of a prior stage of life that haunts you now / deep inside
your cells" can be transformed into beauty.

> Grant Clauser, author of *Muddy Dragon on the Road
> to Heaven*

Gnashing Teeth Publishing
242 East Main Street
Norman AR 71960
http://GnashingTeethPublishing.com

Printed in the United States of America

ISBN 978-1-966075-00-4

Library of Congress Control Number: 2024948897

Non-Fiction: Poetry

Gnashing Teeth Publishing First Edition

Fragmentation and Volta

Table of Contents

Fragments for Ken Smith: 1 1

Crown 1: Crusted Filigree 7

    1. pig roast sonnet 9

    2. post-traumatic sonnet 10

    3. the miller's sonnet 11

    4. sonnet for a crepuscular world 12

    5. projectionist sonnet 13

    6. sonnet for the inner suburbs 14

    7. winter sonnet 15

    8. sonnet to measure language 16

    9. storm sonnet 17

    10. stained glass lights up a sonnet 18

    11. rural sonnet 19

    12. jv football sonnet 20

    13. lighthouse sonnet 21

    14. underwater sonnet 22

Fragments for Ken Smith: 2 23

Crown 2: Swamp Culture 29

    1. sonnet as archetype 31

    2. sonnet for friendship in the workplace 32

    3. sonnet mapped to a grid 33

    4. interstellar sonnet 34

    5. sonnet that only exists in the tropics 35

    6. sonnet on post-coital tristesse 36

    7. sonnet for an abandoned building 37

    8. sonnet for floating 38

    9. sonnet for morning light 39

    10. sonnet for blindness 40

11. sonnet with cables 41

12. sonnet with ocean light 42

13. sonnet for the pastry chef..43

14. language sonnet for cloud systems 44

Fragments for Ken Smith: 3..45

Crown 3: The Bitter Clarity 51

1. rollercoaster sonnet 53

2. sonnet for an ancient religion..54

3. sonnet as memento mori 55

4. angel sonnet 56

5. thanksgiving sonnet 57

6. sonnet for mountain ash..58

7. asphalt love sonnet..59

8. sonnet for a damaged bridge 60

9. sonnet in honor of the postal service...61

10. sonnet for sexual dreaming 62

11. sonnet from a western state...63

12. sonnet for a philosophy of living 64

13. two hearts make a sonnet 65

14. alcoholic sonnet 66

Fragments for Ken Smith: 4..67

Crown 4: The Concept of Future Fruit 73

1. sonnet for the wrong mountains...75

2. sonnet for alternative careers 76

3. dream sonnet with framing 77

4. sonnet for gentrification..78

5. burning landscape sonnet..79

6. sonnet for a sacred trespass...80

7. foggy road sonnet..81

8. metal birds make a sonnet...82

9. sonnet for daily compromise 83

10. sonnet for keeping secrets..84

11. sonnet for the child of rain remembered....................85

12. sonnet for the finding of forgiveness 86

13. sonnet for a dolphin child 87

14. sonnet for leaving new york 88

Fragments for Ken Smith: 5..**89**

Acknowledgments..**97**

Fragments for Ken Smith: 1

… imagine a living creature turned to stone   cold blood and raw meat enclosed in shells made of chitin   a billion tons of which are produced every year   imagine tearing it apart with arthritic fingers   all of this trapped motionless in the flashing light…

…imagine a short man   stubby and powerful   running in the rain glorious cooling rain on a hot day in summer   the woman waiting for him   pregnant in her linen dress   sitting silent in the darkest room of the old house   unaware she must soon be cut free from his memory…

…he understood the usage of flags   and was able to translate their subtle messages   not merely the white flag of surrender   or the green banner of negotiation   but here we see an eagle on an azure field   fish hooked in talons   soaring before darkness falls on the world…

…the cathedral was always the tallest building in the city   until money became the only true god   now the nave is empty as the candles flicker and die   one by one   but even the mightiest spires were nothing compared to the blue majesty of the mountains   shimmering at twilight…

…early in life he had begun to keep a map of all the places he had traveled and all of the places he had been unable to visit   he tracked street names and restaurants   and paid particular attention to the types of flora that grew wild in the major parks…

…she could tell by his eyes that he was drifting away   and by the way the corners of his mouth twitched when he replied to her question   his blood as cold as the lizard silently clinging to the sunbaked wall of the outdoor bathroom   incomplete   like most of his projects…

…there was a route through the mountains   but the path was long and arduous   so many miles of walking and climbing   the local children were happy to act as porters   as long as you did not attempt to photograph them   at which they would melt into the forest…

…the men claimed that their ancestors had been trees   which is apparently unique as an origin story   later when they pulled up their roots from the ground and walked   they would sleep in the dens of foxes hunting small mammals and eating the eggs of birds…

...the words spoken related to the internal shape of the mouth   and to the love that breathed in the spaces between them   this then was the message brought down from the mountain   this then was what was actually known to be true...

...metals related to other metals in much the way that rocks relate to other rocks   things being excavated from the final clearing at the edge of the woodlands   they had been traveling for days when they came to the cornfields   where only husks were still remaining...

...they walked across a plain that seemed to stretch into a formless and colorless purity   a silence that resembled the image of death in a mind that had never faced it   they had an urge to rush home in order to ensure that the children were safely sleeping...

...the return was through a place of wilding confusion   a land once of agriculture   every field long with the swaying grasses that signified a sufficiency   if not a surfeit   but there was a sickness beneath the surface   penetrated deep into the blood...

...they cut the rocks using the tools they had to hand   cut them into blocks more or less oblong which were used to build their permanent dwellings   there were fields beyond   wet from the flooding of the river a highway for their boats to travel on...

...music cannot exist without the concept of waves   pure wavelengths naturally depending on the perfection of materials   wood or brass or steel   a form of communication that incorporates both language and emotion   that is to speech as water is to ice...

...a man dressed as a bird appeared   pigs and dogs squirming around his feet   snails in his hands and pockets as offerings to the chieftains   he had emerged from the desert unable to speak   his calcified tongue incapable of telling his stories of the hidden lands beyond...

...they stopped digging when they came upon the bones   a woman and child   their skeletons intact   though all the flesh had long since perished   once everything was moved and reassembled in the sanctifying darkness of the church   they began their work once more...

Crown 1: Crusted Filigree

1. pig roast sonnet

They all wore black and stank of last week's
Miller Lite   they stank of smoke and memories
they stank of bitterness   that picked up speed
as it tumbled downhill and across the town
before it skidded to a halt in front of the fire
where a pig's head stared vacantly into
the middle-distance   unfocused clouds for eyes
they all wore camouflage as they blended
into suburban life in a small New Jersey town
where cathedral bells were tolling to remind them
of the ones they left behind   in rough pine boxes
buried shallow   or nothing left at all except
the smell of meat and a memory of a face   staring
emptily through the stink of whiskey and pain.

2. post-traumatic sonnet

Staring through the stink of whiskey and pain
following the winding traces on the landscape
of telephone poles   and the threads they carry
the hummingbird signals deep within their
hard-wired casing   every conversation a mystery
every memory a threat to selfhood   the failure
of a prior stage of life that haunts you now
deep inside your cells the knowledge of your
brother who failed to return   a number called
and called again   but never will be answered
perhaps you killed for money or you killed for love
but does it really matter   when blood is on
your hands   remember those days sitting in your
truck in silence while the miller spewed his lies.

3. the miller's sonnet

The miller told his tale   but who knows today
what a miller is or does   who understands
the grinding process   the great stones
and the rushing water of the stream that turned
the wheel that supplied the power to convert
raw grist to fine flour   we live now in
a post-everything world of plastic wrappers
and LED lighting   where children can grow
to adulthood without ever seeing a piglet or a goat
without ever knowing the difference between
wheat and rye   without ever seeing a full moon
reflected in a pond while bats whirl overhead
and the last glimmerings of color from a recently
vanished sun stain the roughness of their hands.

4. sonnet for a crepuscular world

A vanished sun stained the roughness of their hands
as you turned to the door   blue against the red brick
of the wall   walking backwards to watch them
as they sprawled across the stubbled field   pale
as church light in the late afternoon   there had been
rain   and there had been the memory of rain
and there had been days when it seemed the sun
might never rise again   the birds were absent
in that petrifying silence   so many people were solitary
in those days   feeling no necessity for human contact
and you felt lost in a world that crept up on you
a world that was not a place in which you ever measured
time   you stayed in your bed for hours   even though
you realized that eventually you must begin to move.

5. projectionist sonnet

Eventually you knew that you must begin to move
to get out of the rain and into a café   even
if you never took an elevator again   but preferred
instead   to dig into the underground places
that you remembered from certain old movies
from the days when film was projected with light
and heat   into the interchange of space
and motion   where flooded avenues once led
you into the muddied fields of misery
where your friends could only comfort you
while you sat sipping wine   seemingly in a trance
muttering your rosary behind the broken glass
looking for love on the forecourt of a gas
station   still a distance before the city line.

6. sonnet for the inner suburbs

You were still a distance before the city line
where the fires were burning   flames swelling
like an ocean of narrative   Cy Twombly
flower-kissed in orange and red   a desert
blossom that seeds the dreams of a dying planet…
remember the concept of millions   and how
it expanded beyond all limits   remember the shape
as gesture that surrounded the idea of seasons
fading now into unrestricted congruence
it's a time for craftsmanship to resurrect itself
after all these years of specialization   it's time
to work on the shape of our bleeding gums
and the frightful condition of our once fragrant
gardens   where weeds are spreading furiously.

7. winter sonnet

Weeds are spreading furiously across the open
space   not knowing their days are limited
by the impending miracle of winter   that
white-cold death in life that never fails   year
by year and decade by decade   to spread
its crusted filigree across the open water   where
bears and racoons equally partake in the mystery
of seasons   their stories never told   there is
of course no wonder there   that silent dumbness
never thought to generate the thrill which we
ascribe to our own lives   killing time until
a death that barely ripples beyond the thirst
a vulture has for carnage   circling and circling
above the killing fields   lit by a quiet moon.

8. sonnet to measure language

The killing fields are lit by a quiet moon
and here I am in the belly of a god   squeezing words
from a paralytic larynx   shouting out loud that all
poetry is language poetry   someday soon we will
fail to navigate   and existence will end
I check the clock and it's slightly late   and I know
with a sudden intensity that my time has passed
self-pity is corrosive   and this town has no need
of me   there are people sleeping in the streets
frozen on a winter's night   there are homes
that will never be rebuilt   still coated with the mud
of tragedy   the oil and grease of desperation
abandoned to the gods of weather who played
their ace card   rains which fell to a biblical degree.

9. storm sonnet

Rain having fallen to a biblical degree
unstopping for days on end   'till leaving behind
its predictable catastrophe   fields of rotten
items   mud-soaked and stinking of despair
visions seared in survivors' minds of
a subaquatic hell   sunlight's shafts that split
the clouds perceived as mockery   until it was over
and slowly voices began to be heard again
rough hands seen to work themselves to bone
clearing the world of ruin and debris   butterflies
now visible   flying from the mouth of
the apocalypse   working silent to the surface
before erupting from the broken earth
surely to be taken as a harbinger of something.

10. stained glass lights up a sonnet

Taking this as a harbinger of time still to come
these brass and silver memories of childhood religion
tall and bone-skinny in long black robes and white
collar   the choral trills and pocket change
that clinks into the collection plate   blue hair
and crinkled skin   everything observed from
a place of never-sanctioned mockery   the leaves
are falling in the churchyard   horse chestnut fruit
splits open   spilling out the rich brown seed
ancient language on ancient stone that fades
back into forgotten centuries   the stained-glass
windows are dull from outside   but once
within the light spills color   opening up the space
where kind-hearted folks are sitting quietly.

11. rural sonnet

The kind-hearted folks sit quietly   they drink coffee
and listen to the sounds of cattle   and believe deeply
in a specific lack of artifice   haystacks scattered
across the fields that seem to resonate in the blueness
of the morning light   a darkening color with charm
and wistfulness   mapping the rising of the day
to the bracelet that a waitress fingers as she lingers
in her memories   her bones as open as a stream
that drowns a struggling goat   poisoning the day
a simple pathway that follows the contours of the land
that dates back to the depths of history   when native
people followed buffalo across the plaintive width of
nation   it's evening in the city now   time moves faster
there   the sky is a canvas for the towers to shine against.

12. jv football sonnet

The sky provides a backdrop to the towers
silhouetted like a jet plane against a setting
sun   like birds on a wire at twilight
unconvincing in their morphine silence
and there it was that I discovered you   the park
where children would play on the monkey bars
and you   reading literature by cellular refraction
walking to my car through the blazing lights
of junior varsity football   the stink of bergamot
in my nostrils   polishing the trauma of serial
authoritarianism   all I could think of was
the last time we met   when we were both
so convinced of our future   until calamity struck
as soon as we had returned from the lighthouse.

13. lighthouse sonnet

There was nothing else left after we returned
from the lighthouse   no warmth   no personality
a crystallization of colors that froze into place
light seeping from the edges of the cataract
changing how we viewed the world   everything
so cold   everything so blue   the streets
ripped up and replaced with canals   fishermen
casting into shade while dogs slept at their feet
we knew that there must be an ocean   but
didn't know how to get there   sunlight
closing our eyes and stitching our lips together
you whispered sweetly into my ear with syllables
of nonsense   that strung together began to hint
at a deeper understanding than I had ever known.

14. underwater sonnet

It was a deeper understanding than I had ever known
when he disappeared underwater once again   he had
a connection to the depths   he had no fear   and nothing
seemed to fear him   as he cut through entire ecosystems
the light at those depths was pale and mysterious
flickering and temperamental like an opioid dreamscape
the more he swam the more his brain seemed to change
his personality to adapt to ocean life   something had
fused inside him   a new connection   the way the tendrils
of his nerves flowed freely   like seaweed in a sudden
stream of coldness   he rarely spoke of his previous life
of the small town he grew up in   of his father the postmaster
of his mother dead in childbirth   or his so-called friends
from army days   who all wore black and stank of Miller Lite.

Fragments for Ken Smith: 2

…the carpenters pause as the starlings sweep through the tops of the trees immigrant birds not known here in the time of the ancestors   the house they are building will be a quiet place   filled with the hushed murmurings of love and gratitude…

…the air today tastes thickly of ash from the fires that burn half a continent away   they came here to plant   to be farmers   the thick black soil a source of joy   becoming the one fixed star in a constellation of wandering suns in permanent rotation…

…each of them had already lived multiple lives   but not through reincarnation   their existences parallel to each other   the film between them slipping at times into translucency   across the gap the pounding rhythm of the ocean's waves on the midnight shore…

…they dug deeper and deeper but the water was gone   all the wells were dry and the reservoirs empty   he locked himself in the smallest room sealing all the cracks until no air could enter   then lay there as his sweat puddled on the floor   a lake of salt…

…they watched her as she walked down the street   stopping to look in every man's face   it was unclear who she was searching for   it seemed unlikely she would find him in this small town   so few men here   but across the wider world there are uncountably many…

…he had learned to use the light   the glare of it and the shadows that it cast   to accurately categorize the varieties of trees   the shine and polish of their woods   he sang the songs from his glossy black hymn book and left behind those things his erstwhile friends called joys…

…the people in the town had been ignored for so long they no longer had any expectations   they slept on blanket rolls beneath the trees   mornings they hunted scrub jays and orioles   these they trained to sell to travelers who visited the market near the main gates…

…in recent years they had seen birds in the cornfields which once only lived in the depths of the forest   towhees and ovenbirds   for example corpses of small frogs and salamanders were found frozen in winter ice which led to much gossip at all hours of the day…

…he had a dream in which his best friend died   but when he woke he could not remember the cause of it   he was traveling in the south at the time   there was a field of smooth stones   black in the constant rain the wind blowing from the west quietly shunted the cloud masses…

…the rituals of the locals included sand and ocean   fire and blood   they spoke in language unused at other times   a harsh and guttural tongue that provided no space for disagreement   plants were produced   grown in pots in secret dark places…

…the people of the country had learned to listen carefully at all times   it was a subtle action   imperceptible to strangers   but she had gradually learned their procedures   she sat in the shade of a copse of docile trees and wrote copious notes in her journal…

…the streams were depleted   awaiting the arrival of summer rains   in places reeds had choked off the flow and diverted it   cold clear water spilling over its banks   but still in the grip of the mysterious forces that defined the scope and shape of the watershed…

…they had walked through woods until they reached a white house with a wooden deck   men and women sat at a table   drinking and discussing the future   discussing the spread of poison in the fields   the women becoming more intense as the men fell into a stubborn silence…

…once there had been small farms all across the valley   but these had been gradually acquired and merged   unused buildings reclaimed by forest   pine trees hiding the ruins in a thickening darkness that oozed the sweetness of sap   and the loamy spice of good dark earth…

…the sound from the cobbled alleyway seems to be the sound of murder or the hellish screeching of wildcat   as the man upstairs opens his window and rages at the world   as the gull wheels away   a white rag against the empty sea   smoke rising until indistinguishable from cloud…

…the rivers merged after carving shapes into the land at the edge of the city   a grassy place where flat-bottomed boats carried on an undocumented trade   a yellow world at sunrise   snakes sliding through the muddy edges and into the water   as men in uniform roll past…

Crown 2: Swamp Culture

1. sonnet as archetype

What has happened is over and can never be changed
like the loss that is felt from a missing organ   as you
stagger from the public toilet   breathing in the stink of piss
a loud sound still ringing in your ears like the aftermath
of an explosion   tinnitus lingering as you repair to
your bed   nursing the wound in your belly   changing
the dressing and smearing it with salve   washing repeatedly
with purified water   but what really needs purification
is your soul   you realize that now   the sorrow still lingering
long after reparations have been made   long after
you have made the visits   and mailed the checks
trapped beneath your sheets   you listen to the meandering
melody of a solo guitar   that parses time into sheets
of metal   welding a mystery into platonic irony.

2. sonnet for friendship in the workplace

A mystery is welded into platonic irony   sharp metallic
edges   glinting silver in a concrete world   harsh
sounds are magnified   echoing through a cavernous
space   when attempts are made to define the exact
meaning of friendship   parameters mapped as axes
as a graph is formed in n-dimensional space   where one
is always gleaming   edging light through bandwidth
defined as elegy   beyond the wire perimeter you find
a meadow sinking into indigo   as day's end looms
there is still sufficient visibility   cars leave one by one
a delicate dance of compact spacing   home is just
a metaphor for temporary relief   hoping there will be
no rain tonight   because the one thing everyone is sure of
—this grid has been breaking down for decades.

3. sonnet mapped to a grid

The grid has been breaking down for decades
at least since the time of Agnes Martin   who lived
with a lioness when she nailed the universe to
her flattening plane   not lacking in color   not
lacking in a quiet boldness   she traversed a massive
swathe of territory in so many ways   from rural
unchained Saskatchewan to the acid-painted desert
of New Mexico   but always tastefully appointed
as the lights once more began to flicker and fade
as the hum of appliances would suddenly switch
to a nervous silence   and food began to deteriorate
refrigeration releasing its chilling grip   such a waste
as the trash cans fill to overflowing   and maggots
breed and multiply beneath a relentless sun.

4. interstellar sonnet

Maggots breed and multiply beneath a relentless sun
ripe fruit and dead meat   waiting for the cycle to be
halted   waiting for someone to press pause
a world of stink and flies that stays within an immutable
state until you sprinkle it with bleach   will there be
maggots in space   I wonder   will we take them
with us   unknowingly   as we launch our inevitable
explorations   those journeys that will last for many
lifetimes   far beyond this insignificant corner
of the universe   and what will happen to those who
refuse to go   and they will be numerous   how will
they survive the emptiness of a dying planet   leaving
behind the heat and floods of unlivable terrain   fleeing
ever northwards   slipping away from swamp culture.

5. sonnet that only exists in the tropics

It's organic   he says   fleeing into swamp culture
leaving behind the years of espresso and Roquefort
observing the way that light illuminates the mud
that thickens the water   a haven for all types
of menacing organisms   it's fundamental   he
repeats   locked inside a bathroom as refuge from
the hellscape of his family   trying to find a distance
where he might recoil at a non-alarming pace   inside
him is a certain darkness that evades the moonlight
that fails to propagate the shrilling of tree frogs
the screeching of owls   this magnificent heat
even nightfall can never break   a sweat as
pungent as sex   divergent across the infrastructure
of conduit   the taste of nectar on his tongue.

6. sonnet on post-coital tristesse

The taste of nectar was on his tongue   but his feet
were frozen into blocks of ice as he walked through the rain
just another man in a long dark overcoat   a brimmed
hat protecting his head from the weather   a head full
of memories   of oiled torsos slithering and naked
in an overheated room   of breakfast mornings
with coffee and eggs and fresh fruit   driving through
the sunlit valley with the snow-capped peaks all around
and the sound of laughter   the softness of memory
and touch and a heart-bursting tenderness   and then
so suddenly   it was over   and now he walks the city
blocks oblivious to weather   driving his thoughts
like a nail into the firmament   watching it crack and split
apart   rendering into darkness elliptical   darkness pure.

7. sonnet for an abandoned building

Darkness elliptical   darkness pure   wet
from the roots   darkness cellar-bound in crumbling
stones of ash and moss   the doors are locked
but the walls are missing   there are diamonds
trapped in coal dust   while horses stand quietly
in a corner of the field   occasionally flicking
with their tails   they stay away from broken glass
their warm tongues and nuzzling muzzles
taking sugar from a young girl's hand   my tongue
spills darkness and I call it poetry   I call it
birdsong   my head now spinning as I slide
through the place that used to be a wall
no shoes on my feet   slicing open flesh with
diamonds or glass   adding to the earth's moisture.

8. sonnet for floating

I was between the diamonds of the earth's moisture
floating on a raft   on a lake   and I had fallen
into a dream where everything kept disappearing
until I was surrounded by nothing but sky   and then
in my dream   I realized that the sky was in fact
a mirror image of some other sky   or some other
blueness   everything was so pure   and I kept floating
through the pureness   I knew I was only a visitor
here   and up ahead was a rocky shoreline   it was
almost like the beginning of a new religion   I felt
the need to burn candles   forcing their waxen shafts
into the smooth forgiving soil to hold them upright
waiting for the sadness of the time to lead me on   lead me
into a new day   into that particular specificity of light.

9. sonnet for morning light

I've spoken numerous times about the particular
specificity of light   reflected on a given body of water
in motion   I've spoken about the way you appeared
backlit by sunlight   my heart trapped in my throat
both of us locked into the embrace of the land
listening to the rhythmic patterns of wingbeats
to the melodies of birdsong as the first light
glazed the leaves at dawn   both of us sinking
deeply into memory   and how that early light
has nourished us from the distant past   reaching
back to a time before such memories were fixed
were locked into neurons   accessible and indexed
when the locomotive that powers life had barely left
its station   the tracks ahead still curving into opacity.

10. sonnet for blindness

The tracks we followed had barely left the station
through the frost of morning   through
the forest of pine and cedar   beneath us
the wood was rotten with spillage   but the rails
gleamed with a soft curvature of flame that melted
into light   it was the wind holding everything
in place   static raptors poised aloft   while the man
in my carriage was already sleeping   proving
himself unavailable for conversation   or consolation
his systems diverted to the work of generating
dreams   eyelids flickering in sympathy with
an incoherent plot   his blindness no longer
any kind of obstacle   his heart beating violently
so heavy as it was   nearly too large for his chest.

11. sonnet with cables

His heart was too large   weighed heavy
in his chest   attached to cables   once thick
with amperage   he had debarked at the island
many years ago   wasting his time in the gaps
between light and stone   spare cables twined
around his neck   a hi-vis rubber jacket
and shallow boots   the single road ran through
a range of low-slung hills where children clung
tightly to flowered aprons   salt spilled on
their morning sandwich   their open mouths a torch
of melody   a song that groped through seasons
of darkness to a glorious ringing as the gray-
flecked seam of daylight returned   his thread
of consciousness tightening   then falling away.

12. sonnet with ocean light

Consciousness tightens   it falls away   after
the move to the ocean address   fixed within this
density   a souvenir of vacation days   speaking
the shape of words once forgotten   now recalled
painting with pulses of light   there is always
photographic evidence   a deck   a table with
angled edges   the smell of salt in the breeze   a dead
thing near the water's edge   where a metal jacket
had pierced its soul   and all that still remains
is bone   day's end flaring orange   redeeming
darkness until spinning back into morning
the new day dawning pearl   dawning iridescent
the oven overflowing with the odor of breakfast
butter brushed and baked like a winter roll.

13. sonnet for the pastry chef

Winter rolls you like a doughboy   brushed
with butter and ready to bake   some exotic
Austrian pastry perhaps   enough to feed a cavalry
or empty out the graveyard of a monastery
when opioid deaths still pass uncounted along
the length of the old canal   passing shadows
cast by rampant growth bamboo   or any
other less than welcome intruder that spreads
its footprint and claims a place   the Jesuits
don't care   locked as they are in thirst of wisdom
parsing their dreams inside the flat dimensions
of the page   edging towards the fragile membrane
that separates the cream from simple milk
oven ready and only waiting for the crust to burn.

14. language sonnet for cloud systems

Waiting for the crust to burn   there is a sudden change in
the motion of hot air   as it circulates within a factorial space
there is a liquid darkness that builds itself up from the simplest
elements in order to create more complexity of thought
pumping itself up to a fuller   more robust set of functions
that can be used for sophisticated tasks such as aggregation
and summarization   this is not an orthodox use case   though
the house is mostly asleep   staircases have been known
to develop into a helix   and many objects which are internal
can be mapped into objects which are external   such as trees
and clouds   there is a hardening   and a development of
shape   but the clouds are still as white as ever   and light
flashes suddenly across an opening   turning water into vapor
what has happened is over and can never be changed.

Fragments for Ken Smith: 3

...time had been sliced into fragments   and the fragments were individuated   some slid and fell and were lost in the gaps   while others remained in their strength   powerful hands that could tear apart the continuum   they had no clothing   all lost in the empty houses...

...he took his family to the shooting range where they took detailed notes before traveling cheerfully home in the evening in basket-weave vehicles towed by horses   past the ducks who illuminated the pond with the majestic illusion of their color and texture...

...landscape absorbs you with its surface   but you may fail to recognize the mass beneath it   focusing on the pink and white of spring   or the gold and burgundy of autumn   you disembark from your train   missing by seconds the one who boarded on the other track...

...a priest cleans his boots as the sun begins to set   his leather turning from black to oxblood   the stones from his cemetery leaking onto the adjacent moor   pagan mounds and ancient dividing lines   lines that cross the acres of emptiness and fill it with purpose...

…ocean thrashes itself onto rocks that resemble a clutch of dinosaur eggs waiting to be fertilized by the seeds of language   dropped by winged creatures who haunt this darkening coast   and as she watched the process unfold   she softly combed her hair and sang to herself…

…there was a great collection of pottery   stained blue and patterned with medieval subjects   battles and jousting and maids with hair stretching long and fair   and aquatic creatures in tanks maintained at a stable temperature   snails and seahorses and so on…

…mothers and fathers had been buried in different cemeteries sometimes at great distances   making the mourning period hard to manage   some gravestones surrounded by bluebells that carpeted the landscape   others serenaded with endless whispering song…

…the old man kept stones in his many pockets which he would gift to the people he met in the streets   some drab and corroded   many lit with mineral warmth   in his youth he had fished from a boat that left the small dock daily   famed for landing eel and cod…

...the man asked her what she wished for   as if she could give him a simple answer   could she tell him that she wanted a man   not a boy and that she wanted children of her own   and to sleep and dream on a boat under warm sunshine in the middle of the lake...

...he started the car and drove away without a word   his soaked and ruined boots tossed into the back seat as he drove in stockinged feet   he planned out a sequence of lazy days until he reached the center of the nation   somewhere flat with miles of visibility under an endless sky...

...their motto was that even the wolf could plead innocence   and that was how they lived their lives   they had been cut off from their neighbors when the river changed course   and had paid a harsh evolutionary price   their poisoned blood   the stink of dog at sunset...

...the coastal train was crowded with passengers who spoke a dozen or more languages   tracks keeping to the lowlands even when the streets of a town tilted upwards to dizzying heights   all of this lit by the star that shadowed them at a discreet distance...

...and they return to the beginning   starting over again and again never knowing who they had been   or why   sometimes in the northern hills   sometimes in the arid plains of the south   worlds of memory and recognition clustering around the edges of wind and water...

...there was a time when the whole nation forgot how to sleep   nights of panic where a loss of consciousness could only mean death   could only mean a shelf in an ice-cold room   monochrome photos of weathered faces plastered to the walls...

...the man saw himself in the barbershop mirror   a trickle of blood on his cheek   hair shorter then he remembered it   his eyes not showing the fear that engulfed him   and he knew that he must leave   take the stone steps down into the depths of the subway...

...there was a spiral stair that braided round and round inside the tower exiting onto the platform that allowed you to see the world as it used to be streams of forgotten images that whipped by in fast succession as if blown by a wind of crackling static...

Crown 3: The Bitter Clarity

1. rollercoaster sonnet

Yes   I said   yes I have been to Six Flags
Great Adventure   I have ridden the terrifying
rides   bones rattled by each rollercoaster
then rushing through the slug infested lowlands
away from the deathly rictus of the smile I left
behind   with nothing now to say   no point
repeating   left for dead by mean girls and large
boys   but I escaped   embarked upon my journey
to the salt tides of infinity   where damaged children
bleed upon a beach   washed by the quiet waves
a winter sea of crashing ice that layers itself
across an almost silent harbor   the only sound
the screeching of the gulls   their wings as white
as virginity   their heads as black as crime.

2. sonnet for an ancient religion

With heads as black as crime   they are a constant
presence   persistent in their refusal to leave
I can no longer remember when it was that they
first appeared   but their skulls are packed with
my worst moments   my conscience and my
shame   they exist inside the softness of a failing
religion   draped in darkest robes   bursting at times
into a forgotten hymnal   it's all so melodramatic
you might say   it should be easy to ignore
but you are missing the hopelessness of the context
you are missing the terrible ignorance of the world
that created them   and so I yearn for the silence
of a coffin   and a life in death   buried under
the soil where the view can never be appealing.

3. sonnet as memento mori

The view is not great from under the soil
roots piercing the opaque orbs of rotten eyeballs
tissues flaking back into the ochre sludge
of original sin   the river having leached
into granite bedrock   having hollowed out
its caverns   a kind of splendor not available
for those of us with earth forced into our nostrils
our throats jammed full of eggs that surely must
hatch before we get too cold   our skulls
as you imagine   are never as naked as those
that shine with reflected light in an ancient
masterpiece   embedded in chiaroscuro
surrounded by the softly glowing flesh of peaches
angels watching us with their terrible smiles.

4. angel sonnet

Angels watch us with their terrible smiles   their
lives already lived as full as time   standing so
terribly erect on such delicate feet   already
implicated in the knowledge of forever   moving
through this not-life at such an impossible speed
never falling   except in the way that birds fall
deliberately into flight   falling down only to soar back
upwards   crossing and re-crossing the garden beneath
a peach sky of cloud-smoke and blood   a relentless
sky that reflects the storms of winter's ocean
washing across the tallest buildings of the cities
in shadows of hidden iniquity   spiraling out
into the majestic fields   presenting to us a ruined
harvest   straw spilling from their empty hands.

5. thanksgiving sonnet

The stuffed shirt stands erect   straw spilling
from empty hands   thanks given for the morning's
chill   he wears a mask to hide his lack of feeling
painfully aware that this is a time of many
deaths   both great and small   crows flock
around his feet   feeding on the excess seed
vultures swirl above   locking their spirals into
thermal columns   driving to such heights
as can be triggered by convection   our ragged
mendicant believes in progress   in the song
of the lark and the gut-scraping wail of violin
his lifeless days are filled with newspaper
and sentimentality   once again he fails to cast
a shadow   still fearful of the encroaching flame.

6. sonnet for mountain ash

Fearful of the encroaching flame   of the field
that hugs the mountain pass   a burned gray field of
devastation   a fire was stoked   then left to resolve
shining in the bitter clarity of cinder   holding
the space where a tower was once constructed   a lunar
landscape that glimmers under sunlight   as you pause
to catch your breath   still searching for language
to complete the instant   a drum pounding in your
ears   it's as if a kind of love is holding you   trapped
and motionless   but the berries in the trees are red
as blood   hesitation now over you take the winding plunge
drunk on speed alone   an eagle tracking as you flee
this volcanic place   faster and still tighter until you
relax into the cracked gray asphalt of a parking lot.

7. asphalt love sonnet

The cracked gray asphalt of the market lot   simmering
under a midday sun   as cormorants cluster around
a bottle of gin   empty from last night's escapades
it's a suicide street from here to desperation motel   through
three lanes of hot metal   past bloodshot eyes and translucent
skin   the hangnail suffering of the barely alive who sink
slowly into ancestry   their one-time artistry   a distant
memory in these glass-winged days   the pure banality
of chicken fried three ways   the sad mysticism of grocery store
tacos   and out there   somewhere between the smoke-stained
whisper of a renegade saxophone and the legendary
awkwardness of the undercover cop   a space is found
where   in one small corner of shade   two lovers hold
each other with bulldog grip   tearing beauty from silence.

8. sonnet for a damaged bridge

Beauty is torn from silence as the moon dips out
of view   no longer reflected in the stillness
of the shallow creek   no longer lining the branches
of the apple trees with silver   the sudden darkness
impacting   as it must   upon the tiny drama played
out this night   as much as any other   among
those few nocturnal creatures that take advantage of
the interplay of light and cloud   upriver the bridge
still holds its place   stone-heavy and unresponsive
to the high-stepped gait of herons   or the quiet
rumble of the early morning van that comes to a sudden
halt   its beams picking out the hazard sign   this route
still closed from last week's flooding   insult is
now added to injury   as the mail will be late again.

9. sonnet in honor of the postal service

Our mail is late again   I see him down the street
in his pale blue uniform and oversized sneakers
he has big feet   talking to my neighbor the ex-cop
who is quietly sinking into dementia   the mailman
believes in solitude   he wants to slip his
load into your box in silence   a wraith that fades
into the shadows cast by clouds   some days he'd
rather be a gutter man   creeping from rooftop
to rooftop without the need to concern himself
with human interaction   with his ladder strapped
to the roof of his truck   and a set of power tools
to clear the debris from your pipes   the mail is late
again   I see him standing in the street   lost in
a dream of swirling leaves and the roar of machinery.

10. sonnet for sexual dreaming

Lost in the roar of machinery that you hear from
the open window   hidden by trees that filter
the flickering sunlight   is the almost sexual hunger
that you felt in the early morning silence   before
you were fully awake   when your dream somehow
switched from you riding a bicycle down a long empty
street   past a parade of young women who had been
wearing elaborate dresses   but are suddenly naked
and one of them dives into a lake that wasn't there
a minute ago   the water so unexpectedly warm to your
skin   to your own nakedness   and as you step out
of the tub where your boots and jeans are carelessly
scattered   I wait for you beneath the covers   wait
for the feeling of the softness of your body against mine.

11. sonnet from a western state

I love the sensation of you pressed against me   your skin as soft
as glove   we are in some other state where the nights are truly dark
where land is divided by fences that cross the ocean of long grass
beneath an orange moon   there are no tourists here   there are only
machines that poison the pristine world with gasoline and smoke
within this scale   we can recognize our irrelevancy   we are tuned
into the tautness of musculature   our senses the simmer of liquid
after the sun rises   there was frost here   not long ago   and a ram
was trapped in the frozen stream   there is a metal bridge that has rusted
into the decorative   an art derived by chemistry from the surging force
of nature   the house we are renting has six windows   maybe more
nobody has lived here for a long time   we came here to find a place
to bury our grief   we turn on the fluorescent light and boil another kettle
of water   so many things now simplified   even the coffee is instant.

12. sonnet for a philosophy of living

So many aspects have been simplified   as we slide past
another artificial turning point   the planet spinning its circuit
of the sun   we measure from that point   still following the path
we set ourselves   so many years ago   still   for the large part
contented with the life we have created   no paradise
this   and never would we claim it such   not being so foolish
but if life is to be a song   then let it be a joyful song   let it
overwhelm the darkness that defies us   from hideous corners of
this world   we have no religion   no spiritual beliefs to help
us navigate a perfect life   instead we focus on a purely philosophical
intent   a plumb line   that bisects the material and the idealistic
attempting to avoid the egoistic and ungenerous   who we are
exists in language   exists in neurology   and biology
physiologically consistent   my heart and yours   are so alike.

13. two hearts make a sonnet

My heart and yours   alike in myriad ways
the same strong muscle   the porous receptivity
we speak a similar language   hard-edged
at times   yet with a softness ready to take flight
at any moment   delivering on an inner promise
of benevolence   driven by the same belief
in honesty and courage   knowing how the shape
of a life leads to its inevitable end   my hand or yours
the wielder of the cunning blade   stranded in
this empty place between the burning forests
bending flexible   as we dance our stories into
a setting for mythology to dazzle   dressed in
cotton winding sheets   prepared to raise the doors
to light   and sadness   and a glimpse of infinity.

14. alcoholic sonnet

From light to sadness   we glimpse infinity   life
is so often beset by obstacles   forcing us to linger
in the violet depths of shadow   forcing us to commit
the best of ourselves to the terrors of alcohol   nailing
ourselves to the cross of our own misgivings   waving
our goodbyes to friends and family   all who wish
us well   all who might be able to help us overcome
this hurdle   this forced march into the tunnels
of addiction   disguising ourselves in elegant attire
we fall with open eyes into our own trap   acting
as if we are going for a casual stroll through the greenery
but in reality we have nothing to say   no way to save
ourselves   never to be heard from again until we reach
the other side   after we have ridden the terrifying ride.

Fragments for Ken Smith: 4

...hands and face scrubbed clean   he made his way back to the garage empty now of people   just the shadows of machines   oil-slick patches drifting beneath poor lighting   and his betrayer was hidden there   dark-eyed and steel-bladed   teeth glinting with motion...

...the men who survived the failure of media   who fucked their women on stinking couches in the back rooms of poker games   still believing in a world defined by finance   a world of insurance and speculation   a spiraling through accountancy and the odor of stale tobacco...

...in the centuries before light pollution the skies were thick with stars layer upon layer fading back to the origin of the one true infinity   but he sat there motionless in his dark room   tied to a plain wooden chair   a hat on his balding head   an apology on his lips...

...the clinic was closed due to a lack of needles   the damaged ego of policy awash in the fundamental failure of politics   but gulls ate trash in the parking lot   and the contents of a dead hawk's stomach   she was certain that he must be dead   his blood staining her retinas...

…there were no longer any limits after their world was partitioned   each section allocated to a keeper of power   the border areas deteriorated quickly into scrubby grassland   and the locals   who ploughed the fog-stricken bottomlands   became detached from society…

…love was something to be read about in ancient yellowing archives maintained by the bigger libraries   everyone was expected to marry at least three times   and to produce sufficient offspring for the maintenance of wires and fences   and other critical infrastructure…

…their knuckles were bleeding on the silk and lace trim of their sleeves but they took out the day's trash and spent hours making telephone calls to strangers   this effort would somehow dislodge currency   would polish and smooth the gears of industry…

…certain things had been lost in the transition   such as the idea of the warrior   the beauty of a full moon   or the way in which a twice-told lie would become truth over time   people woke up from what felt like a death in life   finding themselves on the streets of a strange city…

...there was a tightness to how she wanted to be held   the feeling was an echo of her own desire   nothing that she had read in a book   either fictional or otherwise   she sat on a mossy rock by the river and watched closely the droplets moving in time to the beating of her heart...

...it was a flat place   the horizon more distant than could be comprehended   people hereabouts raised pigeons   even though they no longer used them for messaging   they had telescopes to watch their doves   as they dipped and soared in magnificent flight...

...he had reached the time in life when he had forgotten more than he still remembered   looking up he saw the river of geese flowing back into the north   brilliant white against the ice-blue morning   as he breathed in the smell of fresh paint   and reconsidered motion...

...the speaker understood that forgiveness was an essential part of bravery and that while ownership of a horse was a necessary stage of development there was more to living a good life   he picked his teeth clean with a twig and began to ascend the ladder...

...it was a small city in the east of the country   where a man might come to learn the skills required to wage a war on behalf of his king   where he might acquire a certain level of fame   be written about and translated into numerous languages   no matter the depth of his loyalty...

...they sat quietly and watched the pale-barked sycamores that grew so immense on the banks of the river   and they remembered their childhoods in the northern lands   when they would play chess together skilled in the slanting strategy of pawn and bishop...

...the cities were burning   the skies above the great plains were dark and acrid   a world now of misery and terror   the children had already forgotten what life was like before   when it was still possible to feel safe in your home   before the battlefields reeked of meat...

...she had written him a series of letters   none of which he had answered but she would not be discouraged   evenings she fed the goats and cattle as the sky rotated through a rainbow of colors before fading to black and then by candlelight she began to write again...

Crown 4: The Concept of Future Fruit

1. sonnet for the wrong mountains

He came from a town of unwilling identity
a town without windows or doors   where
the legs of claw-hammer roosters were encircled
in steel   where death was constantly being
discovered in the underbrush   the excess blood
fattening the midnight worms   still to be spaded
into the crumbling loam by pale-complexioned
dawn-risers   such a textual arena   where words
written on paper could trigger a reinvention of
history   and a slow-moving weather system would
strip the fragrance from the land   don't take
the mountains for granted   this is not Colorado
don't imagine that size can bypass quality   remember
that worth is never exactly equivalent to face value.

2. sonnet for alternative careers

Never accepting things at face value   we remember
a time from before the current time   a time
filled with that which we imagined to be pleasure
even if it turned out to be a mere mirage   and the dream
contained us   locked inside some other role   as
a thinker or an engineer   a dental engineer who
manufactured toothy smiles from resin or acrylic
and we burned bright in the love of our persuasion
in the alcoholic trading of reactions   or stepping lightly
as a dark-cloaked mystic   comfortable among the glowering
faces of men with tall foreheads and perpetual sadness
and we knew that any other life would be less
than this one   touching ourselves to gauge reality
surrounded by stones   engraved with our reputations.

3. dream sonnet with framing

Engraved with our reputations   the stones stand
in a great circle   although none of this is real
we are sleeping   you behind me with your hand
on my belly   your heat and mine combining   our
dreams merging into a new narrative   visible
as crystals under the brilliance of a halogen lamp
a Dylan soundtrack fitfully appearing and fading
from a nearby room   the bed has a metal frame
that can easily turn into a cage   into terrifying fears
of entrapment that dig under the surface of sleep and
contaminate the tales we try to tell each other   outside
in the garden   tomato plants are growing in cages
yesterday they were still green   but in our dreams
we are convinced that tomorrow they will be ripened.

4. sonnet for gentrification

In our dreams we are convinced that the tomatoes
will soon be ripened   we have protected our plants
with a carefully constructed latticework of elegant
cross-hatching   and the concept of future fruit has
navigated the neural pathways from thought to taste
it's a better world when produce is fresh   we buy
new corn and peaches from the farmers market
we grow our own herbs   and an explosion of mint
but the world is creeping up on us   new houses
fill the developments adjacent to the highway
bulldozers continually breaking ground   and all
we can do is wait   humanity is a death cult
it arrives en masse   disguised as the middle class
preaching the gospel of the superior school district.

5. burning landscape sonnet

The middle class arrives   searching for a better
school   searching for a better life   enveloped
in air conditioning   they pay no mind to
the intensity of the heat   the world translated into
a furnace where everything blazes   a carcinogenic
squeal of blackened edges   a pine forest
destroyed   an ashen landscape interwoven
between the golf courses built on cemetery land
all corpses removed for mandatory cremation   their
children blonde and almost naked   beach brats
with futures set   immune to failure   never seeing
the coyotes who cross and recross the boardwalks
their eyes ablaze with the memory of a forest fire
the stench of burning trapped still in their nostrils.

6. sonnet for a sacred trespass

The stench of burning lingered in their nostrils
as they trespassed for the first time on the sacred
lands of the native people   looking for something
that was still unclear   an urge or a fetish   a latent
compulsion that unraveled as they edged deeper into
the last remaining forest   it was light and it was also
dark at the same time   and they struggled to understand
the chemical enchantment that controlled their
drug-addled minds   they could still remember the first
time they read Camus   they still recalled the passion
aroused by the perplexities of existentialism   now
they wanted to live only in the present   they knew
that once they left these woods   the only time they would
feel this real again   would be driving blindly in the fog.

7. foggy road sonnet

Driving in the fog   thinking about what   if anything
we believe in   thinking about a man who is
dying in the ICU   old but not old   a righteous man
in his own way   it's been a hard winter with so much
suffering   it's been a hard decade   even though we
managed to keep the money trickling in   we managed
to keep the candles permanently lit   and the wine cold
and the TV kept the boredom at bay   and when we
needed something more   something different
there was always the car   and the thickening fog
and a wet   winding   road that carved a line
around the spareness of the topology of landscape
a road without any sense of time   darkly discreet
a road that could possibly have taken us anywhere.

8. metal birds make a sonnet

The road might have taken us anywhere   but
instead we are surrounded by birds   white birds
black birds   all are forced out of metal   with
gyroscopes and grease   they manufacture their
myths of predation   I'm feeling even more drunk
than I actually am   as I watch these engines
integrate in swoops of sonic energy   halted within
the magnolia shadow where squirrels are formed
from earth   and fencing   my soul resides outside
in the loamy garden   not in the newspaper columns
where war is exfiltrated   and terminates as sport
not in the sad burning electron streams of broadcast
the bird machines will now proceed to eat my
organs   as the rocks roll slowly back down the slope.

9. sonnet for daily compromise

The rocks roll slowly back down the slope   past
the place where he stands with his crossbow   waiting
for a suitable target   his feelings once again confused
by the combination of the way the light moves across
the landscape   and the memories of that morning
the two of them over breakfast unable to come to
terms with the events of the previous day   and the way
her mother had once again infiltrated their lives
her white hair gleaming like the snow-capped peaks
that he used as a metaphor for what felt he needed to
achieve   not so much the killing   as the living
and a need for something triumphant to break through
the fog of relationship   and family   and the endless
compromises he needed to make to stay safe in her arms.

10. sonnet for keeping secrets

The endless compromises he needed to make
all so that he could keep certain things secret
things that were important to him as well as
to other people   people that he hoped never
to hurt   he had hidden things all around
the house   in desk drawers   on the top shelves
of various closets   wrapped inside old underwear
he was particularly concerned about the girl
never wanting her name to be made public
information   never wanting a sudden milling
of journalists or photographers to appear outside
her door   the pale green door set into the red
brick wall   the garden with the high privet
hedge   all of it feeling like spring all year long.

11. sonnet for the child of rain remembered

It feels like spring all throughout the year   she said
refilling her glass   I'm waiting for something more
extreme   but nobody was listening   which is what
happens when you are a group of three – someone is always
being ignored   and even though there was a beach
outside the window   and views of the ocean   she
sat there motionless   drinking her wine   remembering
when her child was born and how she would bathe
it so carefully   as if it might break   not even assigning
it a gender in her mind   as if it were a toy   not a real
person   and once the child was asleep in its crib   she
would stand there in her nightclothes   watching it sleep
trying to remember the nights when she would walk alone
in the rain   measuring out her breath in tiny amounts.

12. sonnet for the finding of forgiveness

You measure your breath in small amounts   and I
find it hard to sleep now the sun has risen   our
blinds are thin   too flimsy to exclude increasing light
and so I also rise   breakfast and coffee   and the day
is begun   and you as well   you who slept so close to
me the whole long night   sleeping through a not quite
drunk   your eyes drawn to the light   leaving behind
the darkness of your essence   the sadness that still
clings   you walk with me through the streets of this city
into the dark heart where pain and suffering are the stuff
of life   and there we leave an offering   small
and inconspicuous   the way we have always wished
to be   and the sun burns away the veil that filtered our
vision   and once again we find ourselves unbroken.

13. sonnet for a dolphin child

Once again we found our world unbroken   as the sun
shone ever more brightly   and the dolphins leaped gaily
from the silver water   you wanted to catch one   to take
it home and keep it in a pool in the back garden of
the house we didn't yet own   a deep enough pool   salted
to marine levels to save the dolphin's skin from the damage
that freshwater would cause   and perhaps we might
learn to communicate with it   in ways that we could
never communicate with fellow humans   something
more direct   a brain to brain linkage   two species running
in parallel with crossover leakage of thought and information
some years later we might have a child who could swim
with the dolphin in the pool   could become gilled
and aquatic   given time   something new and unheard of.

14. sonnet for leaving new york

I have nothing new to tell you   nothing that is previously
unheard   perhaps that my father was born in February
which could explain some of the colder aspects of his
personality   but does not explain why I fled to New
York City   so many years ago   New York City – a body
without a head   a snarling rhythm of emotion   without
a single guiding principle   and this is where I decided
that I should not grow old   and so I fled again to distant
rural valleys and hills   a quiet place that never tries to
fake its pleasure   like New York City does   a restful place
embedded in zoology   somewhat monocultural   but lacking
dissolution or debauchery   an enduring place that changes
little over the years   where I can be at ease   by the reflective
blueness of a river   in a town of unwilling identity.

Fragments for Ken Smith: 5

...entropy had played its tricks and emptied out all sense of sensibility the axe was sharpened and the wood was cut   and we were living in troubled times as the city boys dug in their heels   unwilling to give an inch to steal a yard   their painted flesh afire...

...food and drink should be followed by a solid hour of sleep   he said don't leave until the stars are out   until the floodlights drench the field of play with luminous glare   then pace the sidelines that were measured to exactly contain the game that's played inside them...

...birds fly swiftly   scraping the surface of the lake   so much better then we at navigation   they arrow with unerring skill while we stumble confused   the terrain around us changing as we observe   things we once recognized are now a puzzle   packaged and beribboned...

...children convinced each other they were grown and set off on their travels   heading up to where ice never melted   the endless white that fooled the eye and made distance impossible to calculate   the long straight asphalt stretching forever onwards...

...they tell you that you can never go back to the land you came from that once the corner is turned there is no longer anything there   any letters that you write will fail delivery   so be prepared for a life of rootless bitterness   and take a stranger to your bed...

...a part time job serving coffee and sandwiches might be a way to pass an empty phase   you're inside with the air conditioning   and there's food to eat   if you are lucky you might even get to wear a uniform   a particular colored shirt or a special hat...

...the weather continues as it has been   seemingly endless days with no change   as he waits by the pool for the person who will make a delivery he's been told this is a once in a lifetime opportunity   there is little availability and it should be seized...

...an officer arrives with a message of extreme urgency   she's sick and needs immediate attention   you'll find her down by the large buildings on the river   their stacks pouring vapor into the atmosphere   everyone who works there in a constant state of high alert...

...the big red dog   belly full of whiskey   staggering through the streets accompanied by the rancid stench of sewage from overflowing gutters yellow teeth grinding   white fists pumping   as his hatred reaches a new level   looking to find the wrong bar...

...he took his friends to an upscale restaurant   a place where the grandsons of generals and admirals might brag about war crimes   before retreating to their apartments   waiting for the mailman to deliver the check that will last them through the month...

...she arrived from a small provincial town where music and dancing were forbidden   where old folks all read the same newspaper   following the implausible adventures of the tuxedo classes   something to despise and aspire to at the same time...

...much time had passed since they became friends for life   and for some that loyalty would fade to irrelevance in a run-down shack on the periphery of a second rate city   others slid through life like light through a one-way mirror   no sense of shame or responsibility...

…everyone is aware by now that things are not going well   even the princes of the realm are jabbering in whatever language they speak among themselves   the problem starting early morning in the far east gradually migrating with the motion of the sun…

…a menial job would pay for his life of writing obscurities   but after appearing in a popular podcast his name was widely seen across the networks   soon there were lines of people outside his store   their goal being to have him bag their groceries…

…it was a time of celebration   a time of sound and color   of music and fireworks   but she was home with a boiling kettle and a jar of honey to sweeten her life   she is absent from the photos of that day   even the ones of her uncles and grandparents…

…the train accelerated through the tunnel and crossed the international border   slicing through the pressure of dead air   I had been reading and was surprised by the sudden emergence into the daylight   passing the colorful gardens of the suburbs   and on to home…

Acknowledgments

As It Ought to Be: Pig Roast Sonnet
Avantappalachia: Sonnet for the Wrong Mountains
Backwards Trajectory: Sonnet with Ocean Light
Bangalore Review: Metal Birds Make a Sonnet
Bennington Review: Sonnet in Honor of the Postal Service
Book of Matches: Sonnet for Sexual Dreaming
Cathexis Northwest Press: Sonnet for a Crepuscular World
Cutleaf: Sonnet that Only Exists in the Tropics, Sonnet for the Inner Suburbs,
Stained Glass Lights Up a Sonnet, Sonnet for Friendship in the Workplace,
Sonnet for Post-Coital Tristesse
DeLuge: Fragments for Ken Smith (excerpt)
Discretionary Love: Two Hearts Make a Sonnet
Feral Journal: Sonnet Mapped to a Grid
Gambling the Aisle: Sonnet for Blindness
Grey Sparrow: Sonnet for the Child of Rain Remembered
Hare's Paw: Sonnet for Daily Compromise
Harpur Palate: Sonnet for the Pastry Chef
Impspired: Sonnet with Cables
Interpret: The Miller's Sonnet
Last Stanza: Dream Sonnet with Framing
Litbreak: Fragments for Ken Smith (excerpt)
Lothlorien: Burning Landscape Sonnet, Thanksgiving Sonnet, Sonnet for
Mountain Ash
MacQueen's Quinterly: Fragments for Ken Smith (excerpt)
Metonym: Sonnet for the Finding of Forgiveness
The Moving Force: Winter Sonnet
New Note: Post Traumatic Sonnet
Otoliths: Underwater Sonnet, Sonnet for Alternative Careers
Panoply: Rural Sonnet
Poetica Review: Sonnet to Measure Language
Ripe Literary: Sonnet as Memento Mori
Sheila-na-gig: Foggy Road Sonnet
Sleet Magazine: Sonnet for a Western State
Stray Branch: Asphalt Love Sonnet, Lighthouse Sonnet, Interstellar Sonnet
Trampoline: Sonnet for an Abandoned Building
White Walls Review: Sonnet for a Philosophy of Living
Willows Wept: Sonnet for a Dolphin Child, Storm Sonnet
Word City: Sonnet for Floating

About the Author

Paul Ilechko is a British American poet and occasional songwriter. He was born in Barnsley in the north of England, and attended Royal Holloway College, University of London, for his Bachelor's degree. He now lives with his partner in Lambertville, NJ. His work has appeared in many journals, including The Bennington Review, The Night Heron Barks, Southword, Stirring, and The Inflectionist Review. He has also published several chapbooks, including *Pain Sections* from Alien Buddha Press, and *This Liquid World*, an e-chap from Voice Luxe.

www.ingramcontent.com/pod-product-compliance
Lightning Source LLC
Chambersburg PA
CBHW072215220125
20749CB00032B/994

* 9 7 8 1 9 6 6 0 7 5 0 0 4 *